Strong Is Your Hold

BOOKS BY GALWAY KINNELL

POETRY

What a Kingdom It Was   *1960*

Flower Herding on Mount Monadnock   *1964*

Body Rags   *1968*

First Poems 1946–1954   *1971*

The Book of Nightmares   *1971*

The Avenue Bearing the Initial of Christ into the New World:
   Poems 1946–64   *1974*

Mortal Acts, Mortal Words   *1980*

Selected Poems   *1982*

The Past   *1985*

When One Has Lived a Long Time Alone   *1990*

Three Books   *1993*

Imperfect Thirst   *1994*

A New Selected Poems   *2000*

Strong Is Your Hold   *2006*

PROSE

Black Light   *1966*

Walking Down the Stairs: Selections from Interviews   *1978*

How the Alligator Missed Breakfast (for children)   *1982*

TRANSLATIONS

Bitter Victory (novel by René Hardy)   *1956*

The Poems of François Villon   *1965*

On the Motion and Immobility of Douve (poems by Yves Bonnefoy)   *1968*

Lackawanna Elegy (poems by Yvan Goll)   *1970*

The Poems of François Villon (second version)   *1977*

The Essential Rilke (with Hannah Liebmann)   *2000*

EDITION

The Essential Whitman   *1987*

GALWAY KINNELL

Strong Is Your Hold

A MARINER BOOK

Houghton Mifflin Company

Boston   New York

First Mariner Books edition 2008

Copyright © 2006 by Galway Kinnell

ALL RIGHTS RESERVED

For information about permission to reproduce selections from
this book, write to Permissions, Houghton Mifflin Company,
215 Park Avenue South, New York, New York 10003.

www.houghtonmifflinbooks.com

Library of Congress Cataloging-in-Publication Data

Kinnell, Galway, date.
  Strong is your hold / Galway Kinnell.
  p. cm.

ISBN: 978-0-544-63093-2 (pbk.)

I. Title.
PS3521.I582S77 2006
811'.54—dc22   2006011292

Book design by Christopher Kuntze

DOC 10 9 8 7 6 5 4 3 2

I am grateful to my friends Josephine Dickinson, Philip Levine, Sharon Olds, and C. K.
Williams for the careful readings they gave to my manuscript. I would like to thank
Michael Collier, Larry Cooper, and my editor Janet Silver, all of Houghton Mifflin.
Margery Cantor and Jenn Keller have given me invaluable editorial assistance. I am in-
debted to the MacDowell Colony, the Rockefeller Foundation's Bellagio Study and Con-
ference Center, and Yaddo for providing me with splendid conditions for writing.

These poems were originally published in the following journals and magazines: *American
Poetry Review:* "Inès on Vacation," "Promissory Note," "Pulling a Nail," "Walnut." *The At-
lantic Monthly:* "Everyone Was in Love." *Beloit Poetry Journal:* "Hide-and-Seek 1933." *The
Massachusetts Review:* "Sex." *The New Yorker:* "Burning the Brush Pile," "Feathering" and
"Field Notes" (published as one poem, "Feathering"), "Insomniac," "It All Comes Back,"
"Ode and Elegy," "The Quick and the Dead," "Shelley," "When the Towers Fell," "Why
Regret?" *Poetry:* "Conversation," "Middle Path," "The Scattering of Evan Jones' Ashes,"
"The Stone Table," "The 26th of December." *Poets & Writers:* "How Could She Not." *The
Threepenny Review:* "Dinner Party." *The Yale Review:* "Pure Balance."

To Bobbie

Tenderly — be not impatient,
(Strong is your hold O mortal flesh,
Strong is your hold O love.)

      —Walt Whitman

Contents

V

The Stone Table

Here on the hill behind the house,
we sit with our feet up on the edge
of the eight-by-ten stone slab
that was once the floor of the cow pass
that the cows used, getting from one pasture
to the other without setting a hoof
on the dirt road lying between them.

From here we can see the blackberry thicket,
the maple sapling the moose slashed
with his cutting teeth, turning it
scarlet too early, the bluebird boxes
flown from now, the one tree left
of the ancient orchard popped out
all over with saffron and rosy,
subacid pie apples, smaller crabs grafted
with scions of old varieties, Freedom,
Sops-of-Wine, Wolf River, and trees
we put in ourselves, dotted with red lumps.

We speak in whispers: fifty feet away,
under a red spruce, a yearling bear
lolls on its belly eating clover.
Abruptly it sits up. Did I touch my wine glass
to the table, setting it humming?
The bear peers about with the bleary undressedness
of old people who have mislaid their eyeglasses.
It ups its muzzle and sniffs. It fixes us,
whirls, and plunges into the woods—
a few cracklings and shatterings, and all is still.

As often happens, we find ourselves
thinking similar thoughts, this time of a friend
who lives to the south of that row of peaks
burnt yellow in the sunset. About now,
he will be paying his daily visit to her grave,
reading by heart the words, cut into black granite,
that she had written for him, when they
both thought he would die first:
I BELIEVE IN THE MIRACLES OF ART BUT WHAT
PRODIGY WILL KEEP YOU SAFE BESIDE ME.
Or is he back by now, in his half-empty house,
talking in ink to a piece of paper?

I, who so often used to wish to float free
of earth, now with all my being want to stay,
to climb with you on other evenings to this stone,
maybe finding a bear, or a coyote, like
the one who, at dusk, a week ago, passed
in his scissorish gait ten feet from where we sat—
this earth we attach ourselves to so fiercely,
like scions of Sheffield Seek-No-Furthers
grafted for our lifetimes onto paradise root-stock.

Everyone Was in Love

One day, when they were little, Maud and Fergus
appeared in the doorway naked and mirthful,
with a dozen long garter snakes draped over
each of them like brand-new clothes.
Snake tails dangled down their backs,
and snake foreparts in various lengths
fell over their fronts. With heads raised and swaying,
alert as cobras, the snakes writhed their dry skins
upon each other, as snakes like doing
in lovemaking, with the added novelty this time
of caressing soft, smooth, moist human skin.
Maud and Fergus were deliciously pleased with themselves.
The snakes seemed to be tickled, too.
We were enchanted. Everyone was in love.
Then Maud drew down off Fergus's shoulder,
as off a tie rack, a peculiarly
lumpy snake and told me to look inside.
Inside the double-hinged jaw, a frog's green
webbed hind feet were being drawn,
like a diver's, very slowly as if into deepest waters.
Perhaps thinking I might be considering rescue,
Maud said, "Don't. Frog is already elsewhere."

It All Comes Back

We placed the cake, with its four unlit candles
poked into thick frosting, on the seat
of his chair at the head of the table
for just a moment while Inés and I unfolded
and spread Spanish cloth over Vermont maple.

Suddenly he left the group of family,
family friends, kindergarten mates, and darted
to the table, and just as someone cried *No, no!
Don't sit!* he sat down right on top of his cake
and the room broke into groans and guffaws.

Actually it was pretty funny, all of us
were yelping our heads off, and actually
it wasn't in the least funny. He ran to me
and I picked him up but I was still laughing,
and in indignant fury he hooked his thumbs

into the corners of my mouth, grasped
my cheeks, and yanked—he was so muscled
and so outraged I felt he might rip
my whole face off. Then I realized
that was exactly what he was trying to do.

And it came to me: I was one of his keepers.
His birth and the birth of his sister
had put me on earth a second time,
with the duty this time to protect them
and to help them to love themselves.

And yet here I was, locked in solidarity
with a bunch of adults against my own child,
heehawing away, all of us, without asking
if, underneath, we weren't striking back, too late,
at our own parents, for their humiliations of us.

I gulped down my laughter and held him and
apologized and commiserated and explained and then
things were set right again, but to this day it remains
loose, this face, seat of superior smiles,
on the bones, from that hard yanking.

Shall I publish this story from long ago
and risk embarrassing him? I like it
that he fought back, but what's the good,
now he's thirty-six, in telling the tale
of that mortification when he was four?

Let him decide. Here are the three choices.
He can scratch his slapdash check mark,
which makes me think of the rakish hook
of his old high school hockey stick,
in whichever box applies:

❑ *Tear it up.*
❑ *Don't publish it but give me a copy.*
❑ *OK, publish it, on the chance that somewhere someone*
    survives of all those said to die miserably every day for lack
    of the small clarifications sometimes found in poems.

Inés on Vacation

We came down the common road
thinking of nothing much. Summer day.
Maud holding one hand. Fergus holding the other.
Familiar arrangement. We came to the honeysuckle.
Bees were going and coming.
No weariness in their drone. Blossoms
bathed in the lush breeze. We were waiting
for Inés to come back to us tomorrow.
Or, if not tomorrow, then tomorrow.

Dinner Party

1

In a dream, as in a dream,
they sit around a round
table, seven of them, friends
of each other and of me too,
including two of my oldest
and closest. They look like
a bunch so loving they have
made it into paradise, as, in fact,
in life, they actually have—so far,
Aristotle would have us add.
Chunks of tiny sakras, bright
with the light drained from
the worldly sky, fulge from
the tips of the waxen stalagmites,
like heads of salamanders
that have wiggled themselves
into the air. At the table
they talk a kind of talk
I know I don't know, sometimes
they smile it, sometimes chuckle
to each other their arrays
of oral finery. At these moments
their ears bunch up in the somewhat
bizarre natural screwiness
of ears at any sudden thrill.

2

In space as yet untracked
by feet of flies, still unpurged
by Pontic waters or by the Ajax

of the love of things earthly,
they look up, and smile.
"This empty chair. It's for you.
Come." Oh my dears. Yes, except
of course I'm only dreaming you,
the impossibility of you, of being
one of you. I can't. They take
the straitjacket off. So what?
The lunatic continues to hug himself.
Across the table I clink
eyeballs with several of you.
Space sings. My ears gaggle. Why?
I'm making you up as I glidder
through the human dream.
Sometimes, rising from my desk
thick with discarded wretched
beginnings, the only way
I know I'm alive is
my toe- and fingernails grow.
Oh what I could have written! Maybe
will have written . . . Tonight
I will work late, then bed,
then up, then . . . then we'll see.
By then the busgirls and busboys
may have already come and lapsed
me into the lapping waters of ever
more swiftly elapsing time, and then
sat me down propped up on a chair,
alone with knife, fork, and spoon
and many bright empty glassfuls of desire.

Hide-and-Seek 1933

Once when we were playing
hide-and-seek and it was time
to go home, the rest gave up
on the game before it was done
and forgot I was still hiding.
I remained hidden as a matter
of honor until the moon rose.

Conversation

For Maud

— *How* old?

— It was completely inadvertent.
 It was more or less late afternoon
 and I came over a hilltop
 and smack in front of me was the sunset.

— Couldn't you have turned around and gone back?

— Wherever you turn, a window
 in a childhood house fills with fire.

— Remember the pennies we put on the track,
 how the train left behind only the bright splashes?

— Everything startles with its beauty
 when assigned value has been eradicated,
 especially if the value assigned is one cent.

— Does the past ever get too heavy to lug around?

— If your rucksack is too full it could
 wrestle you down backwards.

— Does it ever get lighter?

— Yes, when so-called obsolete words start
 falling off the back end of the language.

— Is it easier to figure things out when you're old?

— I once thought so. Once I said to myself,
  "If I could sit in one place on earth
    and try to understand, it would be here."

— Nice thought.

— Yes, but where on earth was I when I thought it?

— Where do you think you might have
  ended up if you had turned around?

— Where the swaying feet of a hanged man
  would take him, if he were set walking.

— Maybe only half of you is a hanged man.

— Conscious mind would be much
  more dangerous if it had more than one body.

— Do you feel a draft?

— It could be a lost moment, unconnected
  with earth, just passing through.

— Or did I forget to shut the front door?

— Maybe a window exploded.

— Have you noticed the lightbulb in the cellar
  blows out about every two months?

— When ordinary things feel odd
   and odd things normal, be careful.

— I like it best when everything's
   doing what it's supposed to.

— Kissers kiss, roofers roof, matter matters.

— Don't forget to call your friend in Des Moines.

— I called him. He said he's feeling good.
   He said he had just finished eating an orange.

— Where would you like to be right now?

— I'd like to be at McCoy Stadium
   watching a good game of baseball.

— I like it when there's a runner on third.
   At each pitch he hops for home,
   then immediately scurries back.

— If it's a wild pitch, he hovers
   a moment to be sure it's really wild
   and then is quick—like a tear,
   with a tiny bit of sunlight inside it.

— Why the bit of sunlight?

— It would be his allotment of hope.

II

Ode and Elegy

A thud. Shrieks. Frantic
wingbeats like a round
of soft applause.
The hawk jumps on top
of the jay knocked to the grass,
presses his wings to the ground,
digs his claws into the jay's
back, chops at the neck,
scattering
blue feathers. Then,
as easily as a green wave
in heavy seas lifts a small boat
and throws it upside down,
still afloat but keel up, so
the hawk flips the jay,
then tears at his throat.

A blue wing wrests itself free, flaps
like a flag crying *I will fight you!*
The hawk stuffs the wing
back down into place,
clamps it there with a foot.
Now jay and hawk stare
at each other beak to beak,
as close as Jesus and Judas at their kiss.
The hawk strikes, the jay struggles,
but his neck breaks, his eyes
shrink into beads of taxidermists' glass.
As a grape harvester trampling out
the last juices of grape, so the hawk

treads the jay's body up and down
and down and up. He places
a foot on the throat and a foot
on the belly, flaps his wings,
repositions his feet, flaps again,

and lifts off, clutching transversely
the body of the jay, which is like a coffin
made in the shape and color of the dead.

Much as in *the décollage à l'américain*
of the Lafayette Escadrille, when
the pilots fly a long time only yards
above the tarmac, to gain speed, then pull back
hard on the joystick, zooming into nearly
vertical ascent, just so
the sharp-shinned hawk, carrying
his blue load glinting in the sunlight
low to the ground, now suddenly
climbs steeply and soars over the tops
of the Norway spruce and the tamarack.

Feathering

Yesterday she took down from the attic
an old lumpy tea-colored pillow—stained
with drool, hair grease, night sweats, or what!
which many heads may have waked upon
in the dark, and lain there motionless, eyes open,
wondering at the strangeness within themselves—
took it and ripped out the stitching
at one end, making of it a sack.

She stands on a bench in the garden
and plunges a hand into the sack and lifts
out a puffy fistful of feathers.
A few accidentally spill and drift,
and tree swallows appear. She raises
the hand holding the feathers straight up
over her head, and stands like a god
of seedtime about to scatter bits of plenitude,
or like herself in a long-ago summer, by a pond,
chumming for sunfish with bread crumbs.

When the breeze quickens she opens
her fist and more of these fluffs
near zero on the scale of materiality
float free. One of the swallows
looping and whirling about her
snatches at a feather, misses, twists round
on itself, streaks back, snaps its beak
shut on it, and flings itself across the field.
Another swallow seizes a feather

and flies up, but, flapping and turning,
loses it to a third, who soars
with it even higher and disappears.

After many tosses, misses, parries, catches,
she ties off the pillow, ending for now
the game they make of it when she's there,
the imperative to feather one's nest,
which has come down in the tree swallow
from the Pliocene. She returns to the house,
a slight lurch in her gait—not surprising,
for she has been so long at play with these
acrobatic, daredevil aerialists, she might
momentarily have lost the trick of walking on earth.

Burning the Brush Pile

I shoved into the bottom of the brush
pile two large grocery bags holding
chainsaw chaff well soaked
in old gasoline gone sticky—a kind
of homemade napalm, except, of course,
without victims, other than boughs,
stumps, broken boards, vines, crambles.

I braced my knees against the next-
to-the-top roundel of the twelve-foot
apple-picker stepladder
and poured diesel gurgling
and hiccupping into the center of the pile,
then climbed down and sloshed
the perimeter with kerosene and sludge.

Stepping back, I touched a match
to the oil rag knotted to the thick end
of a thick stick and hurled it, javelin
style, into the core of the pile,
which gasped, then illuminated:
red sunset seen through winter trees.
A small flame came curling out from either
side of the pile and quietly wavered there,
as if this were simply the way matter burns.
Suddenly the great loaded shinicle roared
into flames that leapt up sixty, seventy feet,
swarming through the hole they had heated
open in the chill air to be their chimney.

At noon I came back with a pitchfork
and flicked into the snapping flames
charred boughs, burnt-off twig ends,
that lay around the edges of the fire
as if some elephantine porcupine had been
bludgeoned on its snout, on this spot,
and then, rotting away, had left a rough circle
of black quills pointing to where it had been.

In the evening, when the fire had faded,
I was raking black clarts out of the smoking dirt
when I felt a tine of my rake snag on a large lump.
I jerked, shook, beat it apart, and out fell
a small blackened snake, the rear half
burnt away, the forepart alive. When
I took up this poor Isaac, it flashed its tongue,
then struck my hand a few times; I let it.

Already its tail was sealing itself off,
fusing shut the way we cauterize unraveling
nylon line by using its own hot oozings
as glue. I lowered it into the cool grass,
where it waggled but didn't get very far.
Gone the swift lateral undulation, the whip-tail,
the grip that snakes bring into the world.

It stopped where the grass grew thick
and flashed its tongue again, as if trying
to spit or to spirit away its pain,
as we do, with our growled profanities,
or as if uttering a curse, or—wild fantasy—
a benediction. Most likely it was trying to find

its whereabouts, and perhaps get one last take
on this unknown being also reeking of fire.
Then the snake zipped in its tongue
and hirpled away into the secrecy of the grass.

Pulling a Nail

In the year of my birth
my father buried this spike,
half in hemlock half in oak,
battered the flat of its head
into the dead center
of the round dent of his last blow.

He would have struck
in quick strokes filled
with inertia and follow-through.
He would have hit at the precise
moment the direction of force
in the hammer exactly lined up
with the axis of the nail.

As friction tightened, he would have
hit harder, striking up
shock waves that struck back
in his elbow and shoulder.

Near the end, when his arm
grew weak and his hand
could barely hang on,
he would have gone
all out and clobbered
the nail, crushed it into itself,
with each blow knocking
off kilter every new tilt of the head.

I hack and scrape
but can't get the hammer's claw
to catch under the rim of the nail,
and I have no nail pull or pry bar.
But looking back in time, I see
my father, how he solved
it when in the same fix:
angling the claw of his hammer
like a chisel, he cozied it
up to the nail head, then taking
a second hammer, smacked
the face of the first, and kept on
smacking it, until the claw
gouged grooves for itself
in the bruised wood and grudged under.
So I do as my father did.

Now begins what could be called
carpenters' arm wrestling, and also,
in this case, transrealmic combat
between father and son.
We clasp right hands (the flared
part of the hammer handle,
his hand) and press right elbows
to the hemlock (the curved
hammer head, his steel elbow) and pull.
Or rather, I pull, he holds fast, lacking
the writ to drag me down where he lies.

A nail driven so long ago
ought to be allowed to stay put,
until the house it serves
crumbles into its ill-fitting cellar hole,

or on a freezing night flaps up
and disappears in a turmoil
of flame and smoke and
blackened bones; or until the nail
discovers it has become
merely a nail hole filled with rust.

A spike driven long ago
resists being pulled—worse
than a stupefied wisdom tooth
whose roots, which have screwed
themselves into the jawbone,
refuse to budge; worse even
than an old pig who hears
the slaughterer's truck pull up
and rasp open its gate and rattle
its ramp into place, and grunts,
and squeals, and digs in.

Slipping for leverage
a scrap of quarter-inch wood
under the hammer, I apply
a methodology I learned from
unscrewing stuck bottle lids:
first, put to it the maximum force
you think you can maintain,
and second, maintain it.

Just as when an earthworm
pulls itself out of a cul-de-sac,
cautious end pulling adventurous end,
stretching itself almost to breaking
until the stuck end starts to come free,

so this nail, stretched and now
starting to let go, utters a thick squawk—
first sound it has made since
my father brought down his hammer
full force on it, adding a grunt of his own,
and thudded it home—and a half-inch
of newly polished steel stutters
out of fibrous matter intended to grip it
a good long time, if not forever.

My fulcrum this time a chunk
of inch board, I pull again, again
raising a chaotic ruckus,
and another segment of bright
steel screeches free.

Helped along this time by
a block of two-by-four lying
on its inch-and-three-quarter side,
I leverage out another noisy half-inch.
At last, standing the block up
on its three-and-three-quarter-inch side,
I pull hard, hold the pressure,
and the entire rest of the nail,
almost too hot to handle, extrudes
in an elegant curve of defeated matter.

It seems I've won.
But in matters like this
winning doesn't often
feel exactly like winning.
It's only a nail, I know,
an earthen bit. Bent.

Very possibly torqued.
And yet my father drove it
to stake out his only hope
of leaving something
lasting behind. See,
there he is now, bent
at his workbench,
in the permanent
gloom of the basement
of the house on Oswald
Street that he built, as he did
everything he did, alone,
probably driving all but a few dozen
of its ten thousand nails himself.

A dark yellowish aura, like
the dead glow of earliest
electricity, unused to being
harnessed, hangs above
his head. He's picking over
a small heap of bent nails,
chucking some, straightening
others back into usefulness
in the rectilinear world.
At this one he pauses.
He lifts it to the light, sights
along it as if he doubts
it can ever be used again.
I take it from his hand just
as he fades out of sight.
In it I can feel the last heat
of our struggle. Thumb
and forefinger hold the nail

to the bench, bent side up,
forming a little wobbling
bridge between then
and now, between me and him,
or him and me, over which
almost nothing of what mattered
to either of us ever passed.
A hammer still floats in the space
he had been standing in.
I pluck it out of the air
and use it to hammer the nail
up and down its length, rotate it
to keep the bent part on top,
hammer it, rotate it,
hammer it, well into the night.
The cellar windows become light.
It is late. I don't think
I will ever straighten it out.

The Quick and the Dead

At the hayfield's edge, a few stalks
of grass twitch. Bending close,
I find the plump body of the vole.
I lobbed him here myself,
after snapping him in a trap to halt
his forays through the flower beds.
He's dead, and yet he lives,
he jerks, he heaves, he shudders,
as if something quickens in him.
Or does something unimaginable happen,
a resolution worse than death, after death?

I prog and tilt him and peer under him
to see why he twitches, and find
he's being buried, by beetles—
bright red or yellow chevrons
laid across their black wings—
carrion beetles, sexton beetles,
corpse-eating buriers who delve
and undergrub him and howk out
the trench his sausagy form settles into.

Now a large beetle spewing at both ends
moils across him, drouking him
in marinating juices. The reek
is heavy, swampy, undoubtedly savory,
luring from afar these several beetles
and also those freeloaders of the afterlife,
the midden flies, who arrive

just in time to drop their eggs in, too,
before the covering of the grave.

The vole by now has dwelt some while
in death, and yet somehow
he still is looking good. Mouth
gaped, teeth bared: uppers
stubby and old-folks yellow, inch-long
lowers curled inward, like uppers
of beavers when they must subsist on soft food.
Scummaging down into a last resting place,
at the last day, when souls go back
to their graves and resume the form
and flesh that once was theirs, this one
could jump and jig, as if freshly risen
from a full night's dead sloom.

When the flies' eggs hatch, larvae squirm
in and out of the eyeholes; in and out
of the ears; in and out of the snout,
which slorped the airy auras
of flowers; in and out of the mouth,
which, even cluttered with bent choppers,
snipped flowers and dragged blossoms
stem-first through gaps in the stone wall—
except for a large peony blossom that stuck
and stoppered the hole for a week
like a great gorgeous cork—while other larvae
wriggle in and out of the anus, like revenant
turds that go in to practice going out.

The last half of the vole's tail
still sticks out, like a stalk of grass,

as if it might be left that way
as camouflage. At the grave's edge
stands a cricket in glittering black,
ogling it all, like a Yankee town father
spectating at a cross-burning.

A larger beetle, the pronotum behind
her head brilliant red, noggles
into view. Pushing the grass down
on either side, she plouters
without pause past the curled teeth
and down into the underroom
of the self-digesting birth banquet
to deposit her eggs and then wait, and later
pick tidbits from the carcass and feed
her hatchlings mouth to mouth, like a bird.

Soon this small plot will be unfindable.
Every blade of grass will look
like a vole's tail, every smither
of ungrassed earth like burial ground,
day won't feel exactly like day, nor night
like night, and in the true night,
when we have our other, more lunatic day,
I may hear in the dunch of my own blood
a distant, comforting, steady shoveling.

But when the human body
has been drained of its broths and filled
again with formaldehyde and salts
or unguents and aromatic oils, and pranked
up in its holiday best and laid out
in a satin-lined airtight stainless-steel

coffin inside a leakproof concrete vault—
I know that if no fellow creatures
can force their way in to do the underdigging
and jiggling and earthing over and mating
and egg-laying and birthing forth, then for us
the most that can come to pass
will be a centuries-long withering down
to a gowpen of dead dust, and never
the crawling of new life out of the old,
which is what we have for eternity on earth.

III

When the Towers Fell

From our high window we saw them
in their bands and blocks of light
brightening against a fading sunset,
saw them in the dark hours glittering
as if spirits inside them sat up
calculating profit and loss all night, saw
their tops steeped in the first yellow
of sunrise, grew so used to them
often we didn't see them, and now,
not seeing them, we see them.

The banker is talking to London.
Humberto is delivering breakfast sandwiches.
The trader is working the phone.
The mail sorter starts sorting the mail.
The secretary arrives, the chef,
the gofer, the CEO . . . *povres et riches*
Sages et folz, prestres et laiz
Nobles, villains, larges et chiches
Petiz et grans et beaulx et laiz . . .

The plane screamed low, down lower Fifth Avenue,
lifted at the Arch, someone said, shaking the dog walkers
in Washington Square, drove for the North Tower,
struck with a heavy thud and a huge bright gush
of blackened orange fire, and vanished, leaving behind
a hole the size and shape a cartoon plane might make

passing through and flying away, on the far side,
back into the realm of the imaginary.

———————

Some with torn clothing, some bloodied,
some limping at top speed like children
in a three-legged race, some half dragged,
some intact in neat suits and dresses,
many dusted to a ghostly whiteness
with eyes rubbed red as the eyes of a zahorí,
who can see the dead under the ground,
they swarm in silence up the avenues.

———————

Some died while calling home to say they were OK.
Some called the telephone operators and were told to
    stay put.
Some died after over an hour spent learning they would die.
Some died so abruptly they may have seen death from in-
    side it.
Some burned, their faces caught fire.
Some were asphyxiated.
Some broke windows and leaned into the sunny day.
Some were pushed out from behind by others in flames.
Some let themselves fall, begging gravity to speed them to
    the ground.
Some leapt hand in hand that their fall down the sky might
    happen more lightly.

———————

At the high window where I've often stood
to think, or to elude a nightmare, I meet
the single, unblinking, electric glare

lighting the all-night lifting
and sifting for bodies, pieces of bodies, a thumb, a tooth,
     anything that is not nothing.

———————

She stands on a corner holding his picture.
He is smiling. In the heavy smoke
few pass. Sorry sorry sorry.
She startles.
Suppose, across the street, that headlong stride . . .
or there, that man with hair so black it's purple . . .

And yet, suppose some evening I forgot
The fare and transfer, yet got by that way
Without recall—lost, yet poised in traffic—
Then I might find your eyes . . .

Sorry sorry good luck thank you.
On this side it is "amnesia," or forgetting the way home;
on the other, "invisibleness," or never entirely returning.
Hard to see past the metallic mist
or through the canopy of supposed reality
cast over our world, bourn that no creature ever born
can pry its way back through, that no love can tear.

———————

All day the towers burn and fall, and burn and fall.
In a shot from New Jersey they seem like smokestacks
     spewing earth's oily remnants.
Schwarze Milch der Frühe wir trinken sie abends
wir trinken sie mittags und morgens wir trinken sie nachts
wir trinken und trinken

———————

They come before us now not as a likeness,
but as a corollary, a small instance in the immense
lineage of the twentieth century's history of violent death—
black men in the South castrated and strung up from trees,
soldiers advancing through mud at ninety thousand dead
    per mile,
train upon train of boxcars heading eastward shoved full to
    the corners with Jews and Roma to be enslaved or
    gassed,
state murder of twenty, thirty, forty million of its own,
state starvation of a hundred million farmers,
atomic blasts erasing cities off the earth, firebombings
    the same,
death marches, assassinations, disappearances,
entire countries become rubble, minefields, mass graves.

Wir schaufeln ein Grab in den Lüften da liegt man nicht eng.

———————

Burst jet fuel, incinerated aluminum, steel fume, crushed
    marble, exploded granite, pulverized drywall, mashed
    concrete, berserked plastic, crazed chemicals, scoria, rot-
    ting flesh, vapor
of the vaporized—draped over
our island up to streets regimented
into numerals and letters, breathed across
the great bridges to Brooklyn and the waiting sea—
astringent, miasmic, empyreumatic, sticky,
air too foul to take in, but we take it in,
too gruesome for seekers of lost beloveds
to breathe, but they breathe it and you breathe it.

———————

The man doesn't look up.
Her photograph hangs from his neck.
He stares at the sidewalk of flagstones
laid down in Whitman's century, curbside edges rounded
by the rasps of wheels of iron and steel:
the human brain envying the stones:
Nie stają się, są.
Nic nod to, myślałem,
zbrzydziwszy sobie
wszystko co staje się.

———————

I thought again of those on the high floors
who knew they would burn alive and then, burned alive.
As if there were mechanisms of death
so mutilating to existence no one
gets over them, not even the dead.

———————

I sat down by the waters of the Hudson
and saw in steel letters welded to the railing posts
Whitman's words written when America
was plunging into war with itself: *City of the world!* . . .
Proud and passionate city—mettlesome, mad, extravagant city!
But when the war was over and Lincoln dead
and the dead buried, Whitman remembered:
I saw battle-corpses, myriads of them,
And the white skeletons of young men, I saw them,
I saw the debris and debris of all the slain soldiers of the war,
But I saw they were not as was thought.
They themselves were fully at rest—they suffer'd not,
The living remain'd and suffer'd, the mother suffer'd,
And the wife and the child and the musing comrade suffer'd.

In our minds the glassy blocks succumb over and over,
slamming down floor by floor into themselves,
blowing up as if in reverse, exploding

downward and rolling outward,
the way, in the days of the gods, a god
might rage through the streets, overtaking the fleeing.

As each tower goes down, it concentrates
into itself, transforms itself
infinitely slowly into a black hole

infinitesimally small: mass
without space, where each light,
each life, put out, lies down within us.

IV

Middle Path

Let James rejoice with the Skuttle-Fish, who foils
 his foe by the effusion of his ink.
—Christopher Smart

In memory of James Wright, 1927–1980

One at a time your feet lift
and slide through the air, and stamp
down in the awkward gait
of someone who has been wound up
too tight somewhere and set down
pointed in two directions,
inner and outer, both at once—

past wind-fallen trees that hold up
their root systems for psychiatric inspection,
past singers who flash the pink of their tonsils,
past cash registers that cry *Treblinka!* when the drawer
     pops open,
past dogs who hoist a leg but dribble on themselves,
past Boeing wings that lower their landing flaps
     and reveal their tiny whirling gears—
everything found a way to show you its insides

in those days when you walked on Middle Path on fire
in the clear idea that it could be done,
but, since speech that expresses trouble
takes going through hell, also afraid
that it could not be done for long.

You of all of us were able
to sit down forever, almost without self,
with pencil and notebook, with second sight,
wherever life and death meet.

Today, this first day of spring,
I can see you stray off Middle Path,
lifting your feet high to clamber through
the last sooted remains of snow and move
among the ancient graves and hunker down
at a headstone and read the chiselings
time and the chemical rains have spared:

Alfred and [effaced]

Age 6   Age 4

Children of [effaced] and Elizabeth [effaced]

Of such is the kingdom of [effaced]

How Could She Not

In memory of Jane Kenyon, 1947–1995

The air glitters. Overfull clouds
slide across the sky. A short shower,
its parallel diagonals visible
against the firs, douses and then
refreshes the crocuses. We knew
it might happen one day this week.
Out the open door, east of us, stand
the mountains of New Hampshire.
There, too, the sun is bright,
and heaped cumuli make their shadowy
ways along the horizon. When we learn
that she died this morning, we wish
we could think: how could it not
have been today? In another room,
Kiri Te Kanawa is singing
Mozart's *Laudate Dominum*
from far in the past, her voice
barely there over the swishings of scythes,
and rattlings of horse-pulled
mowing machines dragging
their cutter bar's little reciprocating
triangles through the timothy.

This morning did she wake
in the dark, almost used up
by her year of pain? By first light
did she glimpse the world
as she had loved it, and see

47

that if she died now, she would
be leaving him in a day like paradise?
Near sunrise did her hold loosen a little?

Having these last days spoken
her whole heart to him, who spoke
his whole heart to her, might she not
have felt that in the silence to come
he would not feel any word
was missing? When her room filled
with daylight, how could she not
have slipped under a spell, with him
next to her, his arms around her, as they
had been, it may then have seemed,
all her life? How could she not
press her cheek to his cheek,
which presses itself to hers
from now on? How could she not
rise and go, with sunlight at the window,
and the drone, fading, deepening, hard to say,
of a single-engine plane in the distance,
coming for her, that no one else hears?

The Scattering of Evan Jones' Ashes

For Judith Jones

Judith moves like a dancer
on sea swells, in a cloud
of the dust of this ardent man
who, as he grew older, more and more
gave himself to his love of poetry.

The airiest of his relics take
to the breeze, the rest fall
of their own loyalty to earth. Each of us
scoops up a handful of this intimate
grit and follows in her wake.

Some fling the ashes, others
sift them slowly through their fingers
as if feeling for something lost. Finally
the bowl, as wide and shallow as
a primitive grail, is empty.

It is as if the Darwin Lime Enterprise
lime truck out of North Danville
had come and done its cloudy work
and had just now pulled away, leaving
the green slopes dusted white.

Now one of us, a tall red-haired boy,
trumpet in hand, comes running.
He lopes across the moat, plunges into the woods,

which open for him and shut behind him.
A minute later he reappears

in the clearing at the top of the hill.
His hair aflame in a ray of sunset,
he puts his trumpet to his lips and blows
the slow solo in each one of us.
Evan's Welsh warrior corgi Maduc,

giving a high-pitched howl, flops
on his back with stubby legs
in the air, and sleds himself head-first
down to the edge of the pond, on grass
quickened and alchemized by Evan's ashes.

The 26th of December

A Tuesday, day of Tiw,
god of war, dawns in darkness.
The short holiday day of talking by the fire,
floating on snowshoes among
ancient self-pollarded maples,
visiting, being visited, giving
a rain gauge, receiving red socks,
watching snow buntings nearly over
their heads in snow stab at spirtled bits
of sunflower seeds the chickadees
hold with their feet to a bough
and hack apart, scattering debris
like sloppy butchers, is over.
Irregular life begins. Telephone calls,
Google searches, evasive letters,
complicated arrangements, faxes,
second thoughts, consultations,
e-mails, solemnly given kisses.

Promissory Note

If I die before you
which is all but certain
then in the moment
before you will see me
become someone dead
in a transformation
as quick as a shooting star's
I will cross over into you
and ask you to carry
not only your own memories
but mine too until you
too lie down and erase us
both together into oblivion.

Shelley

When I was twenty the one true
free spirit I had heard of was Shelley,
Shelley who wrote tracts advocating
atheism, free love, the emancipation
of women, and the abolition of wealth and class,
a lively version of Plato's *Symposium*,
lyrics on the bliss and brevity
of romantic love, and complex
poems on love's difficulties, Shelley
who, I learned later—perhaps
almost too late—remarried Harriet,
then pregnant with their second child,
and a few months later ran off with Mary,
already pregnant with their first, bringing
along Mary's stepsister Claire,
who very likely also became his lover,

and in this malaise à trois, which Shelley
said would be a "paradise of exiles,"
they made their life, along with the spectres
of Harriet, who drowned herself in the Serpentine,
and of Mary's half sister Fanny, who, fixated
on Shelley, killed herself, and with the spirits
of adored but neglected children
conceived almost incidentally
in the pursuit of Eros—Harriet's
Ianthe and Charles, denied to Shelley
and sent out to foster parents, Mary's
Clara, dead at one, her Willmouse, dead at three,

Elena, the baby in Naples, almost surely
Shelley's own, whom he "adopted" but then
left behind, dead at one and a half,
and Allegra, Claire's daughter by Byron,
whom Byron packed off to the convent
at Bagnacavallo at four, dead at five—

and in those days, before I knew
any of this, I thought I followed Shelley,
who thought he was following radiant desire.

Sex

On my hands are the odors
of the knockout ether
either of above the sky
where the bluebirds get blued
on their upper surfaces
or of down under the earth
where the immaculate nightcrawlers
take in tubes of red earth
and polish their insides.

Insomniac

I open my eyes to see how the night
is progressing. The clock glows green,
the light of the last-quarter moon
shines up off the snow into our bedroom.
Her portion of our oceanic duvet
lies completely flat. The words
of the shepherd in *Tristan*, "Waste
and empty, the sea," come back to me.
Where can she be? Then in the furrow
where the duvet overlaps her pillow,
a small hank of brown hair
shows itself, her marker that she's here,
asleep, somewhere down in the dark
underneath. Now she rotates
herself a quarter turn, from strewn
all unfolded on her back to bunched
in a Z on her side, with her back to me.
I squirm nearer, careful not to break
into the immensity of her sleep,
and lie there absorbing the astounding
quantity of heat a slender body
ovens up around itself.
Her slow, purring, sometimes snorish,
perfectly intelligible sleeping sounds
abruptly stop. A leg darts back
and hooks my ankle with its foot
and draws me closer. Immediately
her sleeping sounds resume, telling me:
"Come, press against me, yes, like that,

put your right elbow on my hipbone, perfect,
and your right hand at my breasts, yes, that's it,
now your left arm, which has become extra,
stow it somewhere out of the way, good.
Entangled with each other so, unsleeping one,
together we will outsleep the night."

Field Notes

When we were out at dinner
last night and a dim mood
from the day hung on in me
that neither the quenelles
de brochet nor the Pignan
Châteauneuf-du-Pape
2000 could quite lift,
she disappeared and plucked
out of the air somewhere
some amusement or comfort
and, quickly back again,
laid it in our dinner talk.

When it was time to leave
and she scanned the restaurant
for the restroom, she went up
on her toes, like the upland plover,
and in the taxi home we kissed
a mint from the maitre d's desk
from my mouth to hers,
like cedar waxwings.

When I squished in bare feet
up to the bedroom, I found her
already dropped off, bedside lamp still on,
Theodore Xenophon Barber's
The Human Nature of Birds
lying open face-down under her chin.

Gazing at her I saw
that she was gazing back,
having been sleeping awake
as the tree swallow does.

I went around the foot
of the bed and climbed in
and slid toward the side lined
with the warmth and softness
of herself, and we clasped each other
like no birds I know of.

Our cries that night were wild,
unhinged, not from here,
as unearthly as the common loon's.

Walnut

On the potholed road from the Port
Authority Terminal the Newark Airport bus
sighs up and down as if moguling.
In my experience, motion of this kind
while sitting in a bus often increases
the size of the penis. It does so now.
A mixed sign. In certain operas
the desire for sex and the allure of death
seem to be present just before or just after
each other but occasionally simultaneously.

Consider the love life of the prostate.
During lovemaking this gland, which is,
as doctors like to say, the size of a walnut,
and has very few pleasure fibers in it
but a great many for pain, transmits
the sensation of pain with growing intensity,
until at last, when our walnut can no longer bear it,
the duct opens and semen bursts out and gives
shuddering relief or ecstatic joy, as you like.

Climbing the Pulaski Skyway on a faulty
pneumatic suspension, the bus gasps
and blows and develops a bucking rhythm
that lets me imagine what the fuck-
ing of buses might be like. Minutes later
I find myself thinking the bus moves
like an antediluvian mammal

being shoved to its grave without first
having been fully persuaded its time is up.
Though not kept informed explicitly, the penis
instinctively senses this turn of thought, and shrinks.

Pure Balance

Wherever we are is unlikely.
Our few kisses—I don't know if
they're of goodbye or of
what—or if she knows either.

Neither do I understand why it's
exhilarating—as well as the other things it is—
to know one doesn't have a future,
or how much longer one won't have one.

Future tramples all prediction.
Hope loses hope. Clarity
turns out to be
an invisible form of sadness.

We look for a bridge to cross
to the other shore where our other
could be looking for us
but all the river crossings

all the way to the sea
have been bombed. We look for a tree—
touch it—touch
right through it—sometimes nowhere

is there anything to hitch oneself to
and we must make our way by pure balance.
This is so and can't be helped
without doing damage to oneself.

Why Regret?

Didn't you like the way the ants help
the peony globes open by eating the glue off?
Weren't you cheered to see the ironworkers
sitting on an I-beam dangling from a cable,
in a row, like starlings, eating lunch, maybe
baloney on white with fluorescent mustard?
Wasn't it a revelation to waggle
from the estuary all the way up the river,
the kill, the pirle, the run, the rent, the beck,
the sike barely trickling, to the shock of a spring?
Didn't you almost shiver, hearing book lice
clicking their sexual dissonance inside an old
Webster's New International, perhaps having just
eaten out of it *izle, xyster,* and *thalassacon*?
What did you imagine lies in wait anyway
at the end of a world whose sub-substance
is glaim, gleet, birdlime, slime, mucus, muck?
Forget about becoming emaciated. Think of the wren
and how little flesh is needed to make a song.
Didn't it seem somehow familiar when the nymph
split open and the mayfly struggled free
and flew and perched and then its own back
broke open and the imago, the true adult,
somersaulted out and took flight, seeking
the swarm, mouth-parts vestigial,
alimentary canal come to a stop,
a day or hour left to find the desired one?
Or when Casanova took up the platter
of linguine in squid's ink and slid the stuff

out the window, telling his startled companion,
"The perfected lover does not eat."
As a child, didn't you find it calming to imagine
pinworms as some kind of tiny batons
giving cadence to the squeezes and releases
around the downward march of debris?
Didn't you glimpse in the monarchs
what seemed your own inner blazonry
flapping and gliding, in desire, in the middle air?
Weren't you reassured to think these flimsy
hinged beings, and then their offspring,
and then their offspring's offspring, could
navigate, working in shifts, all the way to Mexico,
to the exact plot, perhaps the very tree,
by tracing the flair of the bodies of ancestors
who fell in this same migration a year ago?
Doesn't it outdo the pleasures of the brilliant concert
to wake in the night and find ourselves
holding each other's hand in our sleep?

Notes

page 4

I believe in the miracles of art, but what
prodigy will keep you safe beside me.

— Jane Kenyon, from "Afternoon at MacDowell"

page 7

The lines "... those said to die miserably every day for lack / of the
small clarifications sometimes found in poems" refer to the following
passage in William Carlos Williams's poem "Asphodel, That Greeny
Flower":

>   It is difficult
> to get the news from poems
>   yet men die miserably every day
>   for lack
> of what is found there.

page 37

>   ... poor and rich
> Wise and foolish, priests and laymen
> Noblemen, serfs, generous and mean
> Short and tall and handsome and homely

— François Villon, from *The Testament*

page 39

And yet, suppose some evening I forgot ...

— Hart Crane, from "For the Marriage of Faustus and Helen"

page 39

Black milk of daybreak we drink it at nightfall
we drink it at midday at morning we drink it at night
we drink it and drink it

—Paul Celan, from *Death Fugue*

page 40

We're digging a grave in the sky there'll be plenty of room to lie
    down there.

—Paul Celan, from *Death Fugue*

page 41

They do not become, they are.
Nothing but that, I thought,
finally secretly loathing
everything that becomes.

—Aleksander Wat, from *Songs of a Wanderer*

page 41

City of the world! . . .

—Walt Whitman, from "City of Ships"

page 41

I saw battle-corpses, myriads of them . . .

—Walt Whitman, from "When Lilacs Last in the Door-yard Bloom'd"

GALWAY KINNELL has been lauded as "one of the true master poets of his generation" by the *New York Times*. Among his many acclaimed volumes of poetry are *Strong Is Your Hold,* which was selected as a *New York Times* Notable Book; *A New Selected Poems,* which was a National Book Award Finalist; and *Selected Poems,* which was awarded both the Pulitzer Prize and the National Book Award. He has also published translations of works by Yves Bonnefoy, Yvan Goll, François Villon, and Rainer Maria Rilke.

Kinnell has previously been named a MacArthur Fellow and the Vermont poet laureate. For many years he was the Erich Maria Remarque Professor of Creative Writing at New York University and was recently a chancellor of the Academy of American Poets.

CPSIA information can be obtained
at www.ICGtesting.com
Printed in the USA
FFOW03n2052180417
34748FF